OSAIN

SANTERIA AND THE LORD OF PLANTS

By Baba Raul Canizares

ORIGINAL PUBLICATIONS
Plainview, New York

OSANYIN

SANTERIA AND THE LORD OF PLANTS

© 2005 by Original Publications

ISBN: 0-942272-85-4

FIRST EDITION

First Printing 2005

Cover Art and Drawings by
Baba Raul Canizares,
except p. 31 by Eric K. Lerner

Original Publications
22 East Mall
Plainview, New York 11803
(516) 454-6809

INTRODUCTION

Elesije (Osanyin), I am lost in the forest,
but every wrong way I take,
can become the right way
towards your wisdom.

The Orisha Osanyin—called "Osain" in Cuba—is one of the most mysterious figures in Santeria. As the god of herbs, plants, and all vegetation, he is totally indispensable to its practice. Yet he somehow manages to remain aloof of Santeria proper, as if he and his devotees formed an allied but separate brotherhood, always ready to assist, but not too willing to allow us to dig deep into Osanyin's mysterious personality. Although he has some paths and avatars, it is as the outrageously disfigured mutant having a single leg, a single arm, and a single eye that he is popular. It is this form that comes to mind when one mentions the name OSANYIN. While some of his avatars have family histories, especially in Africa, where he is often depicted as Orunla's younger brother, Osanyin is not born of anyone. In fact, it is said that he emerged from the earth's vegetation, which is the reason why he is "half a man" so that he may always remember that the earth is his other half.

Osanyin is the personification of the power of healing locked up in herbs, leaves, barks, and roots. He knows all of the secrets of the earth's greenery. On that day in some ideal future when humankind achieves complete union with Osanyin, disease and ailments will no longer be. There can be some form of Orisha worship that doesn't practice animal sacrifice, there can even be some form of Orisha worship that doesn't practice veneration of physical forms, but there cannot be Orisha worship without using herbs and other plants for spiritual and physical healing purposes. Yet, although Osanyin plays such a pivotal role in the religion, his ethos is elusive, his personality remote. Although Osanyin is highly respected, he is not loved in the same way Babalu is loved, or Shango is loved, or even Orunmila who, although somewhat cold and reserved, nevertheless inspires a certain amount of emotional attachment in his devotees. Perhaps it is Osanyin's other-ness that keeps us from knowing him. Among the qualities Osanyin possesses that keep him emotionally distant are the following: his well-known love of solitude; his constant reminder to all who meet him that he is not "one of us"; his strange appearance; his high-pitched, buzzing speech; the fact that he has an enormous ear that is deaf and a tiny one that can hear a pin drop on the surface of the moon; and his total identification with plant life.

There are few Orisha close to Osanyin. These are: Babalu Aye, a disfigured warrior who shares with Osanyin the pain of not being "normal;" Oshosi and Ogun, who live and hunt with him in the forest; and Shango, Osanyin's godson, the person Osanyin loves most. Although described in some texts as a "minor Orisha,"[1] in reality Osanyin is the spirit of Santeria, for whatever is healing, medicinal, curative and holistic in this faith can be summed up in one word: Osanyin. It is derigueur to learn about Osanyin for anyone showing a sincere interest in Santeria.

1
Sacred Stories (Pataki)
About Osanyin

As the god of plants and herbs, the personified spirit of vegetation, Osanyin figures prominently in ethnographer Lydia Cabrera's masterpiece *El Monte* (Miami: Ediciones Universal, 1986), a 700-plus page compendium of medicinal plants and herbs used in Santeria. I'll start this section on sacred stories by quoting from *El Monte*. Lydia Cabrera's informants were some of the most knowledgeable Santeros of her time—from the 1930's to the 1950's. Their wisdom, filtered through her exquisitely lucid writing, makes *El Monte* that rare ethnographic work that is an absolute joy to read.

> All of the divinities are herbalists, but the uncontested Lord of all herbs, the medicine man, the botanist, is Osain.

> Osain-Agguennîye hails from the land of the Ijesa and is the protector and benefactor of the whole world . . . This powerful deity, our own Lukumi Aesculapius, has but one leg, the right one; one arm, the left one; and one eye. One of his ears is huge and deaf, the other tiny yet so sensitive that it can perceive low and distant sounds such as those made by an ant swimming, or the almost imperceptible sound made by a faraway butterfly as her wings rend the wind...Osain, like the Master Tracker Oshosi, is an expert hunter who can maneuver his bow and arrow as well as any two-armed man, and he can run swiftly on his one foot.... Osain has always been a great friend of Shango, to whom he freely and without ulterior motives gave the secret of working with herbs. [Yet, unwittingly, Shango caused his friend's tragedy].

This is what transpired: Osain for some reason disliked Orunla and was constantly doing works against him. Remembering the adage that the lawyer who defends himself has a fool for a client, Orunla went to consult with Shango, a master diviner, who recommended that Orunla do a work with twelve lighted cotton wicks and twelve thunderstones. No sooner had Orunla started his work when Osain, who was out picking herbs to do bad medicine against Orunla, was struck by lightning and almost burned to a crisp..." [2]

The story goes on to say that Osanyin knew his godson had not intended to hurt him, so Osanyin held no grudge against Shango. In fact, in many Santeria houses the two deities are always fed together. Although in Cuba many pataki portray Osanyin as Orunla's antagonist, in Africa he is often described as Orunla's younger brother, as the following story relates:

Osan-in was the younger brother of Orunla, whose full name was Orunmila. Orunmila's mother gave birth to Osan-in when she was already of age, and he was her last child. Orunmila was so much older than Osan-in that he became almost like his father. Orunmila used to send him on errands. He was training Osan-in to cast Ifa as well. One day, he gave Osan-in a machete and a hoe to clear a bush near the house. But when Orunmila came back, he saw his brother crying. He asked, "Why are you crying? You haven't done any work." Osan-in replied, "I don't know why you asked me to cut down all these trees, leaves, grasses, and roots. This one is a leaf of immortality. This one is a leaf that can cure leprosy. This root is good for cough. This one is good for fever. Why should you ask me to cut down these valuable trees, herbs, and roots?" It is believed that Osan-in brought his knowledge of herbs from heaven, that he was born with it. He didn't learn it from anybody.[3]

Commentary: Even in stories such as this one that attempt to place Osanyin within a normal family context, elements of his otherworldliness surface, such as the fact that no one taught him about plants, he "brought this knowledge from heaven." This particular pataki emphasizes the need to conserve natural resources, since we do not know if the next bush we erase from the face of the earth may have turned out to have been the cure for AIDS!

A pataki famous in Brazil relates this story. Osanyin hoarded all plants in a place where only he could reach them. Shango asked his wife Oya to help him get to the green treasure. The ruler of winds shook her ample skirts vigorously, causing a violent storm to erupt. The squall caused all of Osanyin's plants, herbs, and trees to fly out of their protected environment while the hapless Orisha cried out, "Ewe O! Ewe O!" ("My Leaves! My Leaves!"). All of the Orisha began to grab as many of the plants as they could, each claiming ownership over those plants he or she was able to grab. This is why at present each Orisha has some plants that are identified as his or hers, although the real owner of all plants is Osanyin.

Commentary: This pataki explains how the different Orisha all came to possess dominion over certain herbs. In Africa, no Orisha except Osanyin is thought of as possessing herbs, although many are competent and even miraculous herbalists.

Another well-known pataki concerning Osanyin and Orunla describes how, in their early days together, both enjoyed the mischievous cursing of folk using Osanyin's vast knowledge of plants, which he was teaching Orunla. Olofi, the Great Father, envisioned a different path for Orunla and was greatly disappointed by Orunla's frivolous use of magic. So Olofi decided to kill Orunla! Eshu got hold of Baba's plans, however, and he warned Orunla. Shaken by the news of his impending death, Orunla immediately changed his life, becoming the strict, moralistic pillar of decency he is today, a decision that saved his life!

The following pataki from Brazil relates why one must always offer Osanyin tribute before entering the forest.

It came to pass that Oshosi went to hunt in the forest for the first time, but he couldn't find his way out. He kept following a whistle, but each time the whistle appeared to come from even deeper in the jungle. Finally, Exu appeared with some honey, a cigar, some rum, and some money.

"Did you give Osanyin his tribute?" Asked Exu.

"Why, no, I didn't know I was supposed to!"

Exu lent Oshosi use of his goodies--to be paid back with interest, of course. And Oshosi never again made the mistake of entering the forest without propitiating Osanyin.

About Osanyin in Africa, Dr. Wande Abimbola relates the following:

There is no particular story as to why the one-legged Osan-in has only one leg, this is just his nature. He is the divinity of healing. He is a disabled person himself. In Africa, it happens that special people like that tend to be more devoted to medicine . . . .I think this emphasizes how important special people could be in the culture. Many cultures despise and maltreat people with one eye, one leg, hunched backed and so on. In Yoruba culture, they can become important people and are revered. [4]

2
ATTRIBUTES

Necklace: One of the pataki say that Osanyin brought the use of beaded necklaces to the world, therefore, his necklace should contain every conceivable color. Some traditions use green as an obvious reference to Osanyin's link with greenery.

Shrine (igbodu) How initiates honor Osanyin: Osanyin is not "seated" in the same way other Orisha are, and, like Orunla, he never possesses his devotees. All houses in Cuban Santeria accept that there are certain people who are "born with the gift of Osanyin." They do not need any initiation since, like Osanyin, they brought their knowledge from heaven. Many "Osanyinists," however, are also priests of Shango. According to Santero Julio Garcia Cortez. a fundamental Osanyin is made as follows:

2 small deer horns
7 fresh herbs gathered in the forest
7 different pieces of wood (dry wood sticks gathered in the forest)
7 dry roots
One bag dry roasted corn
The legs, tail, and head of a tortoise offered at the time the omiero was prepared
16 small cowry shells that must have been blessed by an Osain man
16 small black river stones which were previously placed inside the bowls of either Shango, Oshun, or Eleggua
One eye and the tongue of a black rooster which had to be sacrificed to Eleggua
7 [red]feathers from the tail of an African gray parrot

Place all of these items inside the receptacle to be used as Osain "house" [sic]. Wrap in red cloth. Package it inside a wooden box.... dig a hole big enough to cover it beside a silk-cotton tree, pour at least one bottle of firewater [aguardiente], honey, corozo lard [palm oil], [7] grains of guinea pepper. Offer a [tortoise], bury and cover it. Let twenty-one days pass; go back, offer a red rooster, light a candle, roll the coconut shells, get the approval. Dig it out, take to the house where it is to be placed.[5]

And here is Lydia Cabrera's version:

A calabash that will serve as receptacle
The head, the heart, and four feet from a tortoise
A large parrot and a small one
A turtle dove
Carcasses of all of these animals must be dried and reduced to powder before becoming part of the Osain calabash's "magic charge"
an "amansa guapo" vine, a "wakibanga" vine, and a "sapo" vine
The tongue and both eyes from a rooster
Seven human teeth to "help Osain talk"
A bow and arrow
Jaw bone from a goat
Piece of bone from a grave, with the name of the person whose bone it was written down on parchment
Some dirt from the gravesite
Seven dimes
Seven live ants
Seven mate seeds
Half a bottle of aguardiente (or Bacardi 151 rum)

Bury calabash filled with all ingredients for twenty-one days by a silk cotton tree, or by an anthill, so Osain can learn to work like an ant.

After this arduous process, Osanyin is hung at least eight feet high either outside or from a high ceiling. [6]

To add a third elder's voice (3 is my lucky number) to this section, let us examine how Don Demetrio Gomez, who was my Palo teacher, would make an Osain.[7]

As god of plants, Ngurufinda, also known in Palo as Sindaula Ndundu and Yembaka Butanseke, called Osain in Lukumi, is very close to every Palero's heart. It is said that Osain began the practice of making magical potions out of plants and storing the potions in gourds and calabashes many, many, years ago. It was a woman who first discovered the secret potions, forcing Burufinda to share knowledge of how to work with herbs with the woman. She in turn promised not to work with herbs while on her menses, a promise she did not keep. Since that time, most Paleros have taboos against giving the Burufinda deity to women. In our house, we make a special Osain for women, called Osain Kinibo, which is kept outside the home and must be hung at a low altitude, less than eight feet.

People born with the gift of working with plants are called "Osainistas" and are usually children of Siete Rayos (Shango), Osain's favorite godchild. It was to Shango that Osain first taught the secret of how to make powerful medicine out of plants and it was he who first kept a gourd filled with a magical potion in his home. Lucero, Zarabanda, Vence Batallas, and the nfunbi are all intimately intertwined with Burufinda/Osain. The Osain we work with in our house is called Osain Aguenegui Agualdo Kinikini, and the way to praise him is with the following mambo:

Oile sai sai babalogwo

Oile sai sai babalogwo

Osain aweneye eli se ko

Ewel'eye Wile `yare obaniwe

A "hanging" Osanyin

Osain eats goats, tortoises, and roosters, especially a type of fighting rooster called "silky." Ingredients for a gourd Osain include deer antlers, soil from at least seven different places, sticks, a tortoise that has been sacrificed to Osain, rain water collected in May, sea water, river water, Catholic holy water, and whole pepper kernels which must be chewed and spat inside the gourd by the tata. The Osain deity also requires bugs, birds, and coins. After the gourd is filled with all these ingredients, it is then taken to a palm tree, where it is buried for six days in order to receive Siete Rayos' and his sister Dada's ashé. By burying Osain for eight days next to Iroko, Tiembla-Tierra, Nana Bukuu, and Aganju imbue it with their power. [Being] kept buried for three days in an anthill gives the Osain deity the blessings of the nfumbis. Burying it for three days in a crossroads gives it power from Lucero. Each time Osain is taken out of the earth a rooster, a tortoise, toasted corn, dry wine, a silver coin, and rum, must be left inside the hole. Also "The Apostles Creed" and the "Our Father" must be recited after each removal of Osain from a burial. This is called "thanking the earth." Some Osains are not made in gourds, but in terra cotta dishes or small iron cauldrons.

The secret powder that gives life to Osain can be kept inside a small bottle, inside an antler, inside a bull or cow horn, or inside a little gourd. Divination determines which will be used. This powder is made out of four feet from a tortoise, two feet from a small parrot, the remains of a large parrot or macaw, the remains of a turtle dove, the following sticks: amansa-guapo, wakibanza, sapo; plus the eyes and tongue of a rooster, seven large ants, seven human teeth which include the two canines, dirt from a graveyard, hair from a dead person, the name of the same dead person written on parchment, seven mate seeds, plus a little rum. All of these ingredients are to be burned to a crisp, the ashes that remain, along with some stuff that didn't burn, is put in a mortar and pestle and ground to a powder. The ensuing powder is a powerful afoshe that is stored in one of the receptacles described above and then placed inside the larger gourd that had been prepared before. On a Thursday, Friday, or Saturday, the whole deity is to be buried along with a large piece of Iroko, sacrificing another turtle at the site. Three weeks later the Osain is ready to be taken out. The Osain is now complete, ready to be hung up high from the ceiling or from a tree in your backyard or patio, a practice I don't recommend because your enemies may have access to this precious nkisi if it is outside.

Shrine (olujo alejo) How non-initiates may begin to honor Osanyin: The best way to honor Osanyin is by growing plants. But not just grow them in an impersonal fashion, but with love and care, as if they were blood of your blood and flesh of your flesh. Make a living altar in a corner of your apartment with plants that, with care, may thrive indoors. If you want to honor Osanyin, nothing else can compare with the growing of plants.

Offerings (adimu): Custard, feathers.

Blood offerings (ebo): Castrated goat, roosters, and parrots.

Characteristics of Osanyin (and of his children): Osanyin is synchretized with St. Sylvester. His feast day is December 31st. Some traditions in Cuba identify Osanyin with St. Joseph (March 19th),

St. Benedict (March 21st), and with St. Anthony the Abbot (January 17th). His children are thought to be level-headed, mature, yet also unconventional and different. All Santeria houses maintain that there are certain people born with "the gift of Osanyin," who require no other initiation than that which they brought from heaven. Born Osanyinistas are easy to determine because they will demonstrate a complete and intuitive knowledge of the curative, poisonous, and nutritional values of each plant. I have a cousin who used to go out to play when he was a little boy and would bring dozens of herbs and weeds from the outside, telling his mother what each one was good for. He was invariably correct. Many Osanyinistas happen to be devotees of Shango. Many Santeria houses in Cuba say only men can have an Osanyin deity. Even in my own lineage, heavily matriarchal, only women past the age of menstruation were allowed to work with the Orisha. The reason men have placed so many taboos on menstruating women is because they are terrified of the awesome power of this monthly blood sacrifice. Menstrual blood is one of the most potent ingredients in magic. Adding a couple of drops of your menstrual blood to coffee that you make for your loved one makes him fall madly in love with you. He will not be able to think of anybody else.

In Cuba, it is said that of all of Osanyin's plants, the most powerful is the Ceiba tree (silk cotton), also called Iroko. It is in the Ceiba tree that Osanyin makes his home. The following paragraphs and recipes reflect Don Demetrio's insights about the Ceiba: [7]

A plant considered more powerful than all others, including the majestic royal palm, is the CEIBA, the stately silk cotton tree. Paleros sometimes call Ceiba tree "munanzo mambe" (house of God). Most Osainistas and Paleros as well give the Ceiba tree a white chicken offering each month. The Ceiba tree is almost never used for evil purposes.

The one exception is the making of so-called ngangas judias in the Palo Mayombe tradition. The pejorative use of the word "Jew" (judia) to imply evil reflects the anti-Semitic sentiments of the dominant

Spanish rulers of nineteenth century Cuba. In reality, most Paleros are not conscious of the offensive nature of the use of this word. I find it interesting that the Jews I know who practice Santeria and Palo have never complained about this, even though I've instructed my godchildren not to use the word judia in its negative context. Since all the other houses continue to refer to "prendas judias" and "ngangas judias," I mention this here as a way of teaching what these are. The Mayombero will bury the prenda that will be used for evil purposes under Ceiba tree's shadow for twenty-one days. At that time, a totally black cat will be made to become enraged, when it is then decapitated, its skull and left back tibia being made an integral part of the evil nganga.

TO GET SOMETHING FROM CEIBA TREE

To gain Ceiba tree's favor, hard-boil sixteen eggs, removing the shell from each. On the eastern side of the Ceiba tree, draw an equilateral cross using palm oil, then place sixteen pennies and the sixteen peeled eggs, one at a time, over the cross. Place each egg on top of each penny, beginning at the head of the cross down to its feet, then from left to right in the horizontal line. Each time you deposit an egg, say out loud a particular petition--it must be the same petition all sixteen times. At the end, say "Father Ceiba tree, grant me this boon in twenty-one days, amen."

TO CALM AN ENEMY

To calm an enemy, boil four eggs until they are hard, peel them, dress them with cocoa butter, almond oil, and Balsamo Tranquilo or oil of cloves. Take the dressed eggs to the Ceiba tree, making the offering to Tiembla-Tierra, whose palace is in the top of Ceiba tree. Tiembla Tierra will pacify the most stubborn soul.

CEIBA TREE

The father of all trees gives solace to all who ask. There can be no nganga without the Ceiba tree, since its stick is the most important of the twenty-one. When walking by a silk cotton tree, believers must always salute it with respect, saying something like "good morning, Father Ceiba tree, bless me, your humble servant, with health and peace, and forgive me if I've unwittingly stepped on your holy shadow." My father used to call Ceiba tree FUMBE. Spirits called "nfunbi" live in the Ceiba tree, where Paleros feed them periodically. These Eshu-like spirits, similar also to the Gede of Vodou, are offered candy on a brand-new plate. The Palero will write his firma (personal ideograph or sigil) on the ground by the part of the tree's trunk that faces east. Along with the candy, the nfumbi are given four peeled hard-boiled eggs, four clear glasses filled with water, coffee, a lit cigar, and some rum. When a vulture rests on one of the Ceiba tree's branches, we Paleros believe it is a sign of Oshun Ibu Kole's favor. This crone aspect of the goddess of sensuality and riches is called Kana-Kana in Palo. The following mambo is to be sung after sunset to the Ceiba tree.

Sanda Narbe

Sanda nkinia naribe

Sanda fumadaga

Ndinga nkusi

Ndiga mundo

Pangualan boco

Medio tango

Malembe Ngusi

Malembe mpolo

Kindiambo kilienso

Guatuka ngusi

Ceiba tree is a natural temple. It is there that we bury our ngangas, our cauldrons, in order to imbue them with enormous power. In places where there are no silk cotton trees, Paleros will travel to places that have them if they are serious about obtaining the greatest amount of power. There are many Ceiba tree trees in the Southern United States. The Seminole Indians worshipped the Ceiba tree under the name "kapok." Osainistas work with the Ceiba tree in many different ways. Its trunk is used in tying down spells. Ceiba tree's shadow serves as a resting place for many spirits that the practitioner can communicate with. Ceiba tree's roots are the home of a powerful spirit called Mama Ungungu, one of many elementals who serve Osanyin. Soil from around Ceiba tree is offered to the orishas Oddua and Aganju as well as to Osanyin. A tea made from Ceiba tree's leaves will open a neophyte's third eye and help her become a spirit medium. The spirit of Ceiba tree can be contacted even if the tree is not present by singing the mambo listed above while shaking a Ceiba tree stick rhythmically in front of the nganga.

THE EVIL EYE

A small piece of Ceiba tree wood hung with a red ribbon by a baby's crib will protect her from the evil eye. Since many of us believe that there is an eternal struggle between the forces of good and the forces of evil, we have a responsibility to learn how to combat evil in order to maximize our happiness and that of our loved ones. The evil eye is a natural manifestation of evil. Knowing that the eyes are the windows of the soul, we can surmise that a perverted, sick individual who has allowed his soul to become tainted with evil will sometimes even unwittingly look at someone and this evil will spill from his soul through his eyes, affecting the person he is looking at in a negative fashion. Because of their innocence, babies are particularly vulnerable to the evil eye and must be protected at all times. Because they are most defenseless while they sleep, babies should not be allowed to be looked upon while they are asleep. If a stranger or a person known for his evil eye compliments your baby, make sure he utters the phrase "may God bless her" right after. Otherwise, you must say to yourself the words "besale el culito, besale el culito, besale el culito . . ." several times. This literally means "kiss his little ass." Why it works, no one knows. Other talismans against the evil eye that work are a piece of jet (azabache), a piece of red coral, or a dog's tooth. Although many Hispanic jewelers in the U.S. claim they sell azabaches, many times they are selling black plastic beads instead. Genuine jet does not shine, can be pierced with a needle, and will stain a white paper black if one runs it across it. Other implements successfully used to ward off the evil eye are garlic, camphor, and a prayer to St. Louis Beltrand (San Luis Beltran). The great Practitioner Andres Petit, founder of the Kimbisa faction of Palo, said there was no more powerful defense against the evil eye than the prayer to San Luis Beltran. He always carried it with him and would write it down for any one who asked. He knew it by heart. Andres also gave my father the following recipe for lowering a fever: Arrange for three people to read the prayer to San Luis by the bed of the feverish person. (The full version of this prayer is available in *The Powers and Magick of Saints* by Baba Adekun from Original Publications.) Each reader must come, read the prayer, and leave without seeing who read before or after. All three must read in turn not more than one hour apart. A little cross made out of basil leaves and holy water from a Catholic church must also be used by the reader, who must sprinkle some holy water on the feverish person while making the sign of the cross over him or her while holding the basil cross pressed between the right index finger and the thumb each time it says to do so in the written prayer.

A special chamba made out of the leaves of Ceiba tree, guara, yaya, tengue, and caja, serves as baptismal water for infants. Babies baptized in this chamba, called Mamba Nsanbi, grow strong and healthy. Let it be clear that infant baptism in Afro-Cuban religions does not make our children members of any church. They will choose if they wish to remain in the religion when they are old enough to make such a decision.

Herbs and plants: ALL HERBS AND PLANTS BELONG TO OSANYIN!

ROADS OF OSANYIN:

Osain Agguenniye; Osain Agguchuiye: From the land of the Ijesa, protector of all vegetation.

Osain Okuni Gwawo Eleyo: An evil road of Osanyin, the poisonous quality of plants.

Osain Aguenegui Aguaddo Kini-kini: Osain's "full name," according to Lydia Cabrera's esteemed informant, Conga Mariate.[8]

Other names related to Osanyin: **Aguendeguende, Awalabanaba**, and **Obololesu** are often mentioned as avatars of Osanyin. Some scholars, and even some elders, mistakenly name Osun, the fourth divinity to make up the "Warriors" group, as a road of Osanyin. As I'll explain in a future booklet dealing with Osun, they are two totally different Orisha. The Fon people of Benin identify their dog-faced god, Aroni, with Osanyin. In Brazil Aroni is thought to be Osanyin's brother, along with Aroni's twin, Aja. In Haiti he is called Ossangue and Papa Loko. In Arara and also in Palo, Osanyin is known as Ngurufinda. In Cuban Santeria, Osanyin is thought to have replaced an older deity, Inle, as god of plants. Others see Inle as the Divine Physician, who makes medicine out of Osanyin's herbs.

Osanyin in Brazil: In Brazil Ossae (Osanyin) has a position equal in importance to his place in Cuban Santeria. As folklorist Sangirardi Jr. has written:

Ossae a uma divindade fundamental. Sem ele nao haveria transe, nao haveria orixas. Porque Ossae a senhor de todas as plantas liturgicas. Plantas para os rituais de iniciacao. Plantas para o bahno . . . que convocam o deuses . . . . Plantas para as mais diversas cerimonias, no barracao on ao ar livre . . . exigidas pelos orixas on indispensaveis ao cumprimento de um rito.

Osanyin is a fundamental divinity. Without him there would

be no trance, there would be no Orisha. For Osanyin is the Lord of all plants used in our liturgies. Plants used in initiation rituals. Plants used in baths to invoke the gods. Plants for the most diverse ceremonies, indoors or out, plants the Orisha deem essential and indispensable to the performing of our rituals.[9]

In Candomble Osanyin is symbolized by an iron staff surmounted by six points, on top of one of which a stylized iron bird rests. This staff may have a stand, or it may be directly "nailed" to the soil outdoors. His day is Saturday, his Catholic disguise St. Benedict.

In a book he wrote on Osanyin, practitioner Anthony Ferreira states:

Osanyin emphasizes ethics and tranquility. He bestows balanced character (iwa) with equanimity and strength to handle stressful conditions. Osanyin is latent creative energy that allows the person to accomplish pre-determined goals in a structured manner.

Among the various cultures on Earth, we encounter special rules and restrictions about handling plants. Rules of abstinence and purity apply to all aspects of Candomble. The priest of Osanyin abstains from sexual contact at least two days prior to the day that he needs to enter the forest to collect the plants. The body has to be clean, and the mind calm.[10]

3
OSANYIN AND SANTERIA'S "CELESTIAL COURT"

Although, as Lord of plants, Osanyin is certainly the most essential Orisha, he is not regal in the sense that Obatala is regal, or Yemaya, or Oshun, or Shango. Of the Royal Orisha—those who had led lives as kings or queens at some point in their journies through existence, only Ogun resembles Osanyin, both being outcasts to a certain point. Babalu is also like Osanyin, marginalized, different, not pleasant to look at. Funny that the person said to be closest to Osanyin's heart is also the epitome of male beauty and a model of royal stance, his bearing being the epitome of monarchial gallantry: Shango.

According to some pataki, it was Shango who inadvertently caused Osanyin's disfigurement, which would make Osanyin's devotion to Shango even more remarkable. I find the lessons in these pataki to be so currently applicable as to be scary. That a disfigured, handicapped man can hold the keys to an entire universe—Yoruba *weltanschauung* cannot exist without plant life—is in itself a remarkable lesson. When you really think about it, nothing can exist without plant life! What a weird, savage ecosystem would be one that emerged without plants! In this case, I can see why in Africa Osanyin is often called the cause of civility because a world without plants would be an uncivilized world by definition!

In her elegant treatise on Orisha and their attributes, *Los Orishas en Cuba*, Natalia Bolivar Arostegui calls Osanyin a MAJOR orisha. In his effort (as badly in need of a good editor in English as it has been in Spanish) *The Osha*, Julio Garcia Cortez calls him a MINOR Orisha. Who is right? Well, Bolivar is not only a practitioner, but a scholar with solid credentials who studied under Lydia Cabrera. Her book, although relying too heavily on *El Monte* (I guess that's not really a bad thing), is well-written and thought-out. Garcia Cortez's book is a hodge-podge of some good stuff mixed in with preposterous notions. (His whole take on Olokun is so far off the mark I can't believe he didn't cut it off from the English version, and I'd love to hear how his Senkepen Oshun became Senpeken Oya in translation!). In seeing Osanyin as a "minor" orisha, Garcia Cortez betrays a bourgeoisie mentality that refuses to see the importance of the marginalized, no matter how much actual power they wield. This is the same type of mentality that views homosexuals as deviants incapable of dealing with the making of an Osanyin deity because only "REAL MEN" are qualified, according to Cortez.

Bolivar, on the other hand, is a militant member of the communist party of Cuba (Lydia Cabrera was a rabid anti-Communist). Although also part of Latin-American aristocracy (she is a descendant of Simon Bolivar, South American liberator who has a country, Bolivia, named after him), her political views must have colored her sensitivities. So she sees this disfigured, unassuming Orisha as what he is: A MAJOR force in the universe. I would say that, prima facie, Osanyin's position in the Celestial Court is significant. When viewed in depth, no court, no bourgeoisie, no proletariat, no aristocracy, and no life can exist without the spirit of plant life.

Osanyin and forest dwelling warriors Oshosi and Ogun.

4
ORIKI OSANYIN; ORIN OSANYIN
PRAYERS AND SONGS TO OSANYIN

Although at the exoteric social functions of the religion, such as bembes, tambores, guemileres, and toques, songs to Osanyin are rarely played, in the esoteric musical performances that must accompany each consecration of either implements or people, the ritual singing of songs to Osanyin is crucial. No necklaces can be blessed unless we sing to Osanyin. No omiero can be made without Osanyin's songs. And no priesthood can be conferred unless Osanyin is sung to. My elder godsister Sandra Ochun gave me some of these suyeres (songs) to publish here, but she made me promise not to translate them or change them. Because I believe these songs are priceless, I've agreed to publish them as she has requested. I've also included here a couple of songs with English translations that were previously published.

SUYERE 1

ewe ikoko koko wa'lese meji soku'ta
(repeat 4 times)

SUYERE 2

*call: Ashe omo Osanyin response: Ewe Aye call: Ashe onto
Osanyin*

response: Ewe Aye

SUYERE 3

Mamura mofi'ye mamura awo oro'ke
(repeat 4 times)

SUYERE 4

Awade omolo shin shin kosile shin shin iworo

(repeat 4 times)

SUYERE 5

Ewe Inle yomi awona meji yomi oshinshin Inle Yomi bekuba yewa Boroma

(repeat 4 times)

SUYERE 6

Osanyin we'le benito bleo Osanyin we'le benito ble akaka okuma. wele'ye we'le we'le benito ble

(repeat)

SUYERE 7

Ashe wewo'ro ade wao `sheweworo ewe dundun

(repeat 4 times)

INITIATION SUYERE
(per Nicolas Angarica) for the instruction of neophytes
Curu curu guedde
Mariwo zain, Ozain, Ozain mbole mariwo
Cururu cururu
Tiggui, tiggui la gbodin ileera tiggui Ewe, Ewe, nireo Ewe,
Ozain welodde ewe ewe nireo ewe Oma welodde oma omanireo
oma ile nireo ile nireo ile
Moje'un ewe, mosaroo, mo'je un ewe mosara
Ewe lovi mi, ewe loya'mi, moje'un ewe mosara

Dadara madaoo dadara mada Ozain samiwo o camawo dadara
mada
Oyinki yinki odaromiko oyinki yinki odaro mi
Oyinki yinki awa okumaoo oyinki yinki odaromi
Be iseisemio bei lai lemi, ewi guio niyeroko ewiwi awa semineo
Mamura mofiyeo mamura awa lode
Bele Benite bleo, bele benite ble, cacacao kuomobeleble
Wewo nikoko egualese meji soku ta
Shikiri wanwan shikiri wanwan awena meji kiwejo
Shere wawo, ewawo, shere ewawo Ozain odundu
Okumas lawa ewe okuma okuma lawa ewe okuma Abera berama,
abera berama, obba dinya lu Ozain Abera berama yeye
Baba fomore Baba fomore Oba dinya lu Ozain Baba fomore yeye
Ile oma yomi, awona oma yegun, ochinchin oma yegun beduba
yewa lo awa.
Tani guiri oka mi oka Baba kini wolokun
Ile oma sanuko. Oguere wewe sanu ko ma'we
Atikola fagururu, atikola fagururu, ifa owe, ifa oma atikola
fagururu
Alafurewa mamakenyo,1'eri ashe kikenye, alafurewa marnakenye,
l'eri ache kikenyi awo

INITIATION SUYERE
(English Translation)
Break the leaves at the head, Ozain will come to be.
Break fresh herbs, dried herbs are no good.
May these herbs serve us well. May Ozain be with the person for
whom these herbs are prepared and with all of us.
The wounded plants are healing my people, I've eaten of the
wounded plants and they benefit me. Everything Ozain gives us is
good.
All I do is good, all I move is good.
I am an elder and all is good.
Good for me and good for my house, herbs are good.
Come now, children, you have worked but little! keep on working

those herbs!
I may be skinny, but I won't give up. In all of these pots, not a stone is cooked.
Heads that are not clear will roll, we are all puppets and brothers at arms.
Year after year, Ozain speaks clear.
Herbs held death back, thanks to Herbs I am an elder.
Baba provides all the pigeons of this world. Baba, let us all fight alongside Ozain.
All houses will turn to bugs, we will turn into bugs, and bugs are not eternal.
Who gives you bread? The same one who gives everyone else bread.
The house and mouth you have is all you have for company.
To fight all revolutions, let our hands stick together. May the Ashe we have implanted in this head be forever strong! [11]

ORIN (per John Mason)

Ti igi, ti igi Alagbo di ye(a) 'ra

With a tree, with a tree, the owner of the medicine pot makes the body sound. [12]

5
DESPOJOS/CLEANSINGS AND SPELLS WITH OSANYIN

Since at least 90% of all cleansings and spells in Cuban Santeria have to do with plants, books could be filled with recipes for Osanyin works. The few that space limitations permit me to include here have all been proven effective by either me or people I trust.

SPELL TO ATTRACT MONEY

Get a large head of garlic and place in a wine glass where a little water has been placed. Sing a song of praise to Osanyin (see previous section). As the garlic head begins to sprout roots, money will come your way.

TO ATTRACT MONEY/FIND A JOB

Bathe in water to which a bunch of parsley has been added, repeat for three days.

TO MAKE SOMEONE SPECIFIC FEEL ATTRACTED TO YOU

Place five fishing hooks in a small bowl or glass, along with the name of your intended written 0n parchment or brown-bag paper. Fill with honey, yellow rose petals, and jasmine oil. Light a nine-day yellow candle to Oshun.

OSHUN'S (AND OSANYIN'S) OWN
PRESCRIPTION TO ATTRACT A LOVER

As proof of Osanyin's importance to almost every spell in Santeria, when Cuba was in crisis in October, 1962, and flowers, particularly roses, were nowhere to be found, it was widely reported that this spell had no effect. When roses again became available, the spell continued to deliver, upholding its reputation as one of the most reliable of love spells. You can substitute practically anything in this recipe and you may have success, but do it without Osanyin's contribution and your spell will be a disaster!

Here's the recipe. Bathe in water to which a splash of five different colognes and five teaspoons of honey, as well as five yellow roses (petals only), have been added. Repeat for five consecutive days, or do it one day per week for five consecutive weeks, whichever feels most comfortable for you. If a specific person is intended, keep that person in mind while bathing. Do remember that these spells work well only with people who would be attracted to you anyway. A person who despises you may be made to be with you through use of Santeria's magic, but such unions tend to be sad and forced, without joy or spontaneity.

TO MAKE SOMEONE DO SOMETHING FOR YOU

Write the name of the person from whom you desire a favor on a piece of parchment or brown-bag paper, place inside your right shoe under your heel. Go ask your favor while chewing on a cinnamon stick. (Again, without the cinnamon, the spell is useless!)

TO GET RID OF BAD LUCK

Pass a bunch of babies' breath flowers over your body, take it to a crossroads and throw it on the pavement. Say: "As I throw this away, may Eleggua get rid of my streak of bad luck."

Working with Osaynin's tools.

TO KEEP AWAY THE EVIL EYE

Draw or paint a large eye, about 5" by 7", on a parchment or piece of brown paper. Open a prickly-pear cactus leaf in half (they look like pancakes with attitudes), then pierce with an old knife. Put the whole thing in a bag and hang it behind front door. Do not let anyone see what's inside the bag. If you know of a particular person who is talking about you, get another piece of prickly pear, cut it in half through the thin part, giving you two flat pieces. Write the name of person on parchment paper or brown paper. Place the paper in the middle of the two prickly pear halves. Put an old knife you don't mind discarding through both halves. Bind them with a red ribbon—if you are attracted to Shango; a red and black ribbon—Eleggua; or a multicolored ribbon—Osanyin. Tie the ribbon around cactus using a counter-clockwise motion. If Shango is to help you, nail the cactus on a tree—preferably a palm or a silk cotton—with the knife. Leave a bunch of bananas for Shango at the foot of the tree. If it is Eleggua, leave the trabajo (spell) at a crossroads, leaving three pennies for Eleggua as an offering. If Osanyin is to help you, leave the trabajo by a grove or forest along with some white custard and seven pennies.

FOR IMPROVING ONE'S LUCK

The following is a major spell for improving one's luck. It should be done under the protection of Osanyin, Oya or Eleggua. Wear such a ridiculous costume as to make people laugh at you. This could be bright red socks and black shorts—Eleggua—or multi-colored ribbons in your hair—particularly effective if you are a male. Do not tell anyone why you are wearing such funny attire. As people laugh at you, they will unwittingly be washing away your bad luck.

TO BRING A STRAY LOVER BACK

To make a loved one come back after he has left you, take a pumpkin and hollow it out, keeping the top as a lid. Take five nails from the feet of a rooster and put them inside the hollowed pumpkin, adding an egg, marjoram, the name of the loved one written on parchment paper and any personal item you may have of the person you want back. Spit inside the pumpkin three times, then close the pumpkin using the lid. Place the pumpkin next to Mama Chola Wanga or under your bed for five days, then offer it to the river along with five pennies. Your stray lover will come back within twenty-one days.

THE UNIVERSAL CLEANSER

Stronger than Holy Water, your own urine is the most powerful psychic cleanser available. First urine in the morning is thought to be especially powerful and beneficial. Put a little in the water used to clean your home—very little so that its odor does not become noticeable—and add leaves of the pride of India (china berry) tree, the most powerful home-cleansing plant. This powerful combination, this dynamic duo, Osanyin's chinaberry and your pee, will rid your home of negative vibrations. If someone has tried to put an evil spell on you, evidence of which can be a strange powder at your door, an animal carcass, or any unusual object which appears on your doorstep, urinate on it before throwing it out. Sometimes an enemy or someone you dislike will attempt to ingratiate himself with you by giving you a present (such as a piece of jewelry) which you suspect has been "worked." If that happens, urinate on it before you wear it. It will render the working null.

MEDICINE BAGS

For keeping away the police: Burn tips of three buzzard (vulture) feathers along with three dried-up chili peppers. Collect the resulting ashes. Place them in a little black bag to carry with you at all times.

For protection from nosey agents: Toast three shamrock and three witch hazel leaves, grind to a powder, and keep in small black pouch.

To attract lovers: Gather benzoin, valerian, roses, sunflowers, and camwood. Grind all ingredients. Keep in blue, lavender, red, yellow, or pink bag.

To protect against psychic attacks: Keep a small piece of root from an orange tree in a white bag.

To always win court cases: Gather white chalk, cinnamon, white sugar, yellow rose petals, cigarette ashes from a judge. Put all ingredients in a blue bag.

To attract good luck: Combine rosemary, bay leaf, camphor and seven crab's eye seeds and place in a red bag.

6
SOME TRADITIONAL USES OF COMMON HERBS

ALOE: Used in rituals to call Jupiter down. For indigestion. Its gelatinous part is used to soothe sunburn and to help heal small lacerations.

ANISE SEEDS: As a tea, it calms nerves.

BASIL: In Santeria, the most often used herb to ward off evil. In Europe, thought to be the Devil's herb. Witches use it as protection. Beds of basil are thought to be breeding grounds for scorpions.

BAY: A bay tree keeps away evil spirits. It also keeps its owner safe during storms. In Santeria, it is said to bring protection from evil and to bring good fortune.

CASHEWS: When hanging from a string around the waist, they help shrink hemorrhoids.

CLOVER: Provides protection against evil. It has been long held to be a symbol of the Christian trinity.

FERN: Carrying the seed of the fern is said to make the bearer invisible.

GARLIC: It protects against spells, vampires, and the Evil Eye.

LILLIES: These delicate white flowers, when boiled, provide a terrific tonic for weak hearts.

LINDEN FLOWERS: As a tea, it acts as a soporific.

LOTUS: Symbol of creation and fertility.

MARJORAM: As a tea, it helps bring about overdue labor in pregnant women. Also a mild sedative.

MANDRAKE: A painkiller and sleep-inducer, ingredient of many witches' brews. Used in imitative magic because of its resemblance to the human form.

PARSLEY: Thought to bring the blessing of money. In Europe, associated with female practitioners.

PEONY: Said to be of divine origin, it keeps one safe in storms and is an amulet against epilepsy. Widely used in Santeria for its many beneficial uses.

ROSE: Symbol of beauty and love, also of death! A girl who wears a rosebud plucked during Midsummer's Day to church on Christmas Day will meet her future husband within a week.

ROSEMARY: Wards off diseases brought about by magic. In a bath, it brings money

RUE: Keep a plant around the house and no evil can befall you or those under your roof.

SAGE: Its tea gets rid of any headache.

TAMARIND: Its fruit helps digestion, also helps with constipation. A tea made from the bark of the tree serves as a diuretic.

VIOLET: Its leaves and petals serve as natural analgesics.

WATERMELON: Its seeds are ground and mixed with water to serve as a natural "water-pill" (diuretic). Boil its leaves, drain and cool the resulting tea. Pour on your eyes to refresh them. Drink as a mild stimulant.

ENDNOTES

1. As an example see Julio Garcia Cortez. *The Osha* (Brooklyn, NY: Athelia Henrietta Press) p. 182.

2. Lydia Cabrera. *El Monte* (Miami: Ediciones Universal, 1986) pp. 71-72. My translation.

3. Wande Abimbola. *Ifa Will Mend Our Broken World*, (Roxbury, MA: Aim Books, 1997), p. 73.

4. Ibid, p.74.

5. Julio Garcia Cortez, op cit., p. 184-186.

6. Cabrera, op. cit., P.104.

7. Excerpts are from the original publication *The Book on Palo: Wisdom of Don Demetrio*, edited by Raul Canizares.

8. Cabrera, op cit., p.102.

9. Sangirardi Jr. *Deuses da Africa a do Brasil* (Brasilia: Civilizacao Brasileira, 1988) p.101. My translation.

10. Anthony Ferreira. *Esu Osanyin* (Brooklyn, NY: Athelia Henrietta Press, 2000) p.43-D.

11. Nicolas Angarica, *Manual de Orihate* (Havana: Self-Published, 1955) p. 26 A bootleg version is widely available.

12. John Mason and Gary Edwards. *Black Gods, Orisha Studies in the New World* (Brooklyn, NY: YTA, 1985) p.40.

Appendix
Osanyin in Your Bathtub

Herbs and water go together like birds of a feather. It should not be a surprise that one of the ways Osanyin bestows his grace is through the medium of the bath. Following is a list of herbs and their effect on baths.

Alfalfa: Is an excellent herb to use for wealth and prosperity. Works best in not-too-hot water.

Almond: An aphrodisiac when two about to "love" bathe jointly!

Allspice: Increases feelings of well being and love for all things.

Aloe: Enormously popular in Semitic societies, the aloe plant has strong associations with Muhammad. It is said to bring success, love, and protection to the user. Applied topically, it is an excellent soother of hurt skin.

Angelica: Belongs to St. Michael the Archangel.

Anise: Brings love, pleasant dreams, and youthful vigor to wearer.

Balm: Romans added it to their baths as an aphrodisiac.

Basil: Mix with nothing but Florida water, for basil is an herb that works best alone. It brings good vibrations to the home.

Bayberry: Attracts money.

Bay leaves (laurel): Makes you immune to psychic attacks. You should also light a white candle in the bathroom while taking the bath. Read 83rd Psalm before entering water for maximum effect. It also helps with money problems and a weakened constitution.

Betony: Restores physical health; keeps away evil spirits.

Blackberry: Powerful ingredient in baths to repel evil.

"OZAÍN"

A Guzman interpretation of Osaynin.

Blessed thistle: Used to invoke the god Pan and as an aphrodisiac.

Bloodroot: Protects against hexes; uncrossing agent. BEWARE: CAN BE TOXIC! USE MINUTE AMOUNTS.

Caraway: Initiatory baths usually include this plant as an ingredient. It brings good luck to newlyweds.

Catnip: Calms and blesses the bather. Also has aphrodisiac effects.

Cayenne: Induces sobriety.

Cedar: Attracts money.

Calendula: Conducive to peaceful sleep; makes your dreams come true.

Calamus root: Increases attractiveness

Chamomile flowers: To draw money and love. Ancient Romans used Chamomile as an eyewash to relieve ocular strain.

Cinnamon sticks: For love and gambling luck.

Cinquefoil: Keeps away evil entities. Was one of the ingredients in witchcraft's famous flying ointment.

Clover: Repels evil spirits.

Cloves: Bring peace to the home. Gives you power over others.

Coltsfoot: A healing herb.

Comfrey root: Insures your physical safety while you travel.

Damiana: Add to your bathwater to bring sex to your life.

Dandelion: Makes wishes come true.

Dill: Improves your general health when added to bathwater.

Dragon's blood reed: Add to your bath water to help you solve legal problems.

Elder: A powerful herb of divination and protection from all sorts of evil.

Elecampane: An herb of initiation and psychic protection.

Eucalyptus: Helps to get rid of bad habits or evil companions.

Fennel: Protects from hexes. Gives sexual power.

Galangal root: Add to your bath to win a court case.

Garlic: Protects against energy vampires and evil spirits.

High John the Conqueror root: For money or sex, depending how it is worked.

Honeysuckle; For love and good fortune.

Hops: Cures insomnia.

Hyacinth: Add to any love bath. It works well for gay men.

Hyssop: Perhaps the most well-known bath-herb in the African American Christian community is Hyssop, mentioned in Psalm 51 of the Bible as the herb to use for purification from sin. Very strong "stripper" of bad energies. It should be used with care in baths, but works very well in floor washes. For baths, use only a small quantity and do not stay in the bathtub more than eight minutes, for hyssop can cause headaches if too much of it is used for too long a time.

Irish Moss: Brings good fortune.

Jasmine: Acts as an aphrodisiac.

Lavender: Brings a high vibratory frequency to your psyche; increases your psychic powers.

Lemongrass: Brings love to your life.

Lettuce: Brings clarity and calm. Also wealth.

Lemon Balm: Brings love to your life.

Little John Chew: Add a little to your regular bath water to unhex any minor curse you may be experiencing. It also brings general good fortune.

Low John the Conqueror Root: Add to your bath water to attract wealth.

Mandrake: Aphrodisiac; psychic enhancer; uncrossing agent.

Marigold: Natives of Mexico use it as a visionary aid.

Mint: Brings a sweet, happy, vibration. Also, a mild aphrodisiac. May not be strong enough for serious energy-depleting attacks. Use as a floor wash before parties to ensure peace and joy.

Mistletoe: An aphrodisiac.

Nettles: Albertus Magnus recommended using oil of this plant with oil of houseleek to attract fish.

Nutmeg: Add three to your bath water to bring you luck in games of chance and the stock market.

Orris: Brings peace.

Queen of the meadow: Long a favorite bath additive, it brings good **luck.**

Patchouli: Protection; uncrossing.

Parsley: Great for attracting wealth. With milk, it also serves as a spiritual restorative. May not be strong enough to fight a very powerful vampire.

Purslane: Brings money and the protection of the Mother Goddess.

Rasberry Leaves: Increases a woman's attractiveness.

Rose petals (white): Excellent bath to keep your aura strong. Eight roses are needed to provide the necessary strength to fight a vampire. Even if you do not feel you are under attack, take this bath once per week, on Thursdays, as a preventive measure.

Rosemary: Brings good fortune, but may not be strong enough by itself to stave off an energy vampire's attack. Mix with bay leaves.

Rue: Gather the rue in front of you by your altar (if you have one). Light a purple candle and, putting your hands over the rue, palms touching the herb, say: "In the name of God the Father, his power the Shekinnah, and their offspring the Christ, I compel this rue to be ruth, eliminating the ruthless. By the secret name of God, Adonai-EloimYaweh-Amen." Use some in your baths and floor washes to keep evil away.

Saint John's Wort: An herb of protection dating back to the early Greeks; an effective anti-depressant, even as a bath.

Sage: Works better burned than in baths. Use in baths if specifically told to do so by a spiritual practitioner or if you were told to do so in a dream. It increases your wisdom.

Sea lettuce: Keep some in a jar full of alcohol, then use a bit of the alcohol in your bath to bring you peace of mind and good luck.

Slippery elm: Adding it to your bath water keeps people from gossiping about you.

Snake root: Boil a handful for fifteen minutes, then throw away solids and keep liquid in a bottle for seven days. On the eighth day, add it to your bath water to make you attract wealth.

Thyme: Attracts good spirits, uncrosses.

Valerian: Purifies the aura.

Vervain: Excellent for keeping away psychic attacks.

Violet: Fresh, dried, or its oil. Brings good spirits, heals the body.

Willow: In Europe, an herb of eloquence; in China, a source of magical protection.

Witch hazel: In Santeria, a cleansing herb.

Wormwood: Fry some wormwood powder in butter, add a pinch to your bath water as a protector against curses.

Yarrow: This herb is said to increase the human potential for expressing and understanding love.

SOME USEFUL TIPS: When you have decided which herbs to use in your bath, make sure you say a short prayer thanking Osanyin for the use of his herbs, as well as any other orisha who may have dominion over a particular plant. Then place a few cents (odd number) with you in the bath water. Take out a gallon of the water before you enter it. Save it as a floor wash and hand wash if applicable.

If you pick the herbs yourself, a simple ritual you should follow consists of the following. Spray rum in all four directions, then cigar smoke. Say "Osanyin, Baba, ago to ni l'ewe Osanyin, Baba. Moforibale, ashe-o ire-o, Ashe!" Always leave a few pennies wherever you take some leaves or any other part of the plant!

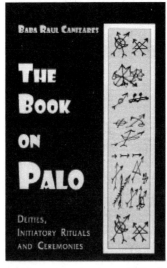

Item #806
Price: $21.95

THE BOOK ON PALO
Deities, Initiatory Rituals & Ceremonies

BY BABA RAUL CANIZARES

Guanabacoa is a city in Cuba famous as the birthplace of some of the most powerful Paleros ever. One of these spiritual giants was Demetrio Gomez, who for nearly fifty years led one of the most potent Palo houses in Cuba. Using an insider's knowledge as well as the careful scholarship that has come to identify his work (Cuban Santeria: Walking with the Night), Demetrio's godson, Baba Raul Canizares, known in Palo circles as Tata Camposanto Medianoche, gives us Demetrio's own teachings, which makes this the best Palo book in English, featuring never-before published sygills, workings, and the unique contribution to the field of over 200 translations of herbs, sticks, and palo sticks from CUBAN Spanish to Bantu and English, including each plant's scientific classification. The book also features' many photographs of rituals, initiations, and sacrifices shocking in their complete honesty.

HELPING YOURSELF WITH SELECTED PRAYERS VOLUME 2

Now With 170 Prayers!

The prayers from Volume 2 come from diverse sources. Most originated in Roman Catholicism and can still be found in one form or another on the reverse of little pocket pictures of saints, or in collections of popular prayers. Another source for these prayers is the French Spiritist movement begun in the 1800's by Allan Kardec, which has become a force in Latin America under the name Espiritismo. The third source, representing perhaps the most mystical, magical, and practical aspects of these prayers, is found among the indigenous populations where Santería has taken root.

These prayers will provide a foundation upon which you can build your faith and beliefs. It is through this faith that your prayers will be fulfilled. The devotions within these pages will help you pray consciously, vigorously, sincerely and honestly. True prayer can only come from within yourself.

TOLL FREE: 1 (888) OCCULT - 1

ORIGINAL PUBLICATIONS